Purnell's World of COMPUTERS

by Peter Bramhill
Illustrated by Graham Smith

ISBN 0 361 05959 0
Copyright © 1984 Purnell Publishers Limited
Published 1984 by Purnell Books, Paulton, Bristol,
BS18 5LQ, a member of the BPCC group.
Made and printed in Great Britain by Purnell and Sons
(Book Production) Limited, Paulton, Bristol.
Typesetting by Quadraset Ltd

Photo credits
P. 10/11 British Science Museum:
Jacquard: British Crown Copyright. Science Museum, London.
Babbage: Photo: Science Museum Collection.
Hollerith: Photo: Science Museum Collection.
Abacus: British Crown Copyright, Science Museum, London.
EDSAC: Computer Laboratory, Cambridge University.

P. 44/45 Robin Kerrod
P. 48, 52 Science Photo Library
P. 42, endpaper: IBM

The Publishers wish to thank the following for
reference material: IBM, British Caledonian, Digital
Equipment Ltd., ICL, Fiat UK, Ordnance Survey.

Front Endpaper: A bit chip magnified.

CONTENTS

About This Book

This book is an introduction to the ever-growing world of computers. Look around you, in your home or school, in your town or in the countryside. Everywhere you can see computers at work, shaping the way we live.

Sometimes the computer may be hidden in a familiar everyday object, like a washing machine in the kitchen or behind the dashboard of a car. In other cases the computer may be more obvious. You can see a computer screen at work in a travel agents, for example, as an assistant checks your holiday booking.

Are you wearing a watch? Chances are that there is a tiny computer inside it!

If you go into almost any high street newsagents you can see books and magazines on computers. Increasingly you can even buy small computers in toy shops, sports shops, department stores and specialist shops.

Everyone has played games on a computer but there are lots of other jobs that they are used for. If you have ever wondered how they work, how to use them and how to write a computer program then read on.

What are Computers?

A computer is actually a collection of different electronic devices linked together. Control circuits allow information in the form of electronic signals to be moved between the different units. Each unit can do a simple job — for example, comparing two numbers or sorting names into a sequence. Together the components work faster than human thought and much more accurately. Once set up to work in a particular way by a person called a 'computer programmer' the machine will work tirelessly.

A home microcomputer is very similar in many ways to the big computers used in industry and commerce. Whatever their size, all computers are made of the same building blocks, although the big computers are more complex in their details. When you buy a home 'micro' it needs to be connected to other units; for example, a T.V. set and a tape recorder. Together these add up to a workable 'computer'.

At the heart of every computer, whether it is a home micro or a large business machine, is the 'CENTRAL PROCESSING UNIT' [CPU]. It controls and coordinates all the different operations of the computer. Inside the control unit the computer's instructions, or 'program', are carried out one by one until the program finishes. The CPU is made up of three parts: the control unit, the logic unit [ALU] and the memory, or store.

The ALU is like a calculator. It is where the computer does its work, where numbers are added or subtracted and where the computer sorts out one piece of information from another.

The memory is where the computer keeps its program and stores data. There are two sorts of memory inside the CPU: ROM and RAM. ROM (read-only memory) contains the computer's master program and you can't usually change it. RAM (random access memory) is quite different. Here the computer can over-write the contents with new information and when you switch off the computer it is likely that the data in the RAM will be wiped out.

The CPU is usually made up of 'chips'. A chip is a small wafer of silicon. The chip manufacturers etch thousands of electronic circuits into one silicon chip. There are usually lots of chips in the CPU, but where one chip contains all the CPU devices it is called a 'microprocessor', a sort of super chip.

There has to be a way of getting data in and out of the computer. A home micro will have a keyboard and possibly joysticks and a light pen. These are examples of 'input' devices.

'Output' devices are used to get information from the computer. Special T.V. monitors and attached keyboards are called 'Visual Display Units' (VDUs). They can be seen in a wide variety of places. The most widely used output device is a printer. Printers range from small units less than the size of this page to huge free-standing ones that produce thousands of lines of print-out per minute.

How it all Began

Most people imagine that Computers are a very new invention. Well, they've been around in one form or another since the Second World War (1939–45) but only in the last twenty years have they become commonplace in industry and commerce. From about 1980 they have been small and cheap enough to become popular in the home and office.

Mankind has grappled with mechanical and logical problems over the centuries, seeking ways to invent machines which could take away some of the drudgery of working things out. One of the earliest calculating devices is the abacus. It is still in use today but was invented in Asia many centuries ago.

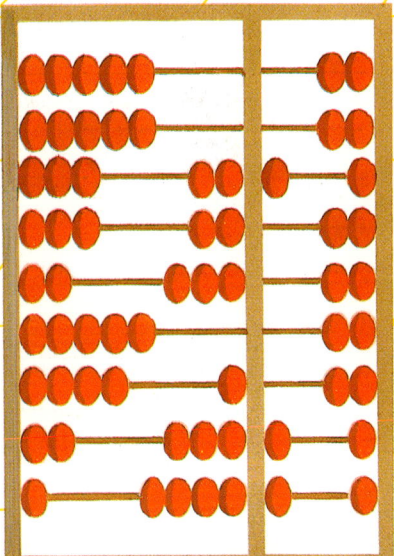

On an abacus the operator counts up to 10 units using the beads on one side of the centre crossbar. He moves the beads on the other side of the bar to record the 'tens' already used.

In 1642, a nineteen-year-old man named Blaise Pascal helped his father to keep the accounts for a shop in France. Blaise made a small counting device which added up numbers using toothed wheels like a gear wheel. As the 'units' wheel turned a full circle so the 'tens' wheel would move one notch round. This is still the principle behind today's mechanical counters, such as the cyclometer.

These early devices could be used to help someone do simple arithmetic but one of the most important features of a modern computer is the operator's ability to program it to do a particular job. Another Frenchman, Jacquard, developed an early form of programming in 1802 He won a competition to invent a simple weaving loom which would produce patterns. He used the method of punched cards to control the pattern on his loom.

In the 1880's an American named Herman Hollerith developed the idea of punched cards further by using them as a method of sorting and counting data. His company was later to grow into IBM. Today IBM is the largest computer company in the world.

In England a Victorian genius called Charles Babbage invented a mechanical computer in 1834 His developments were never finished because he didn't have enough money

Portraits clockwise: Pascal's calculating machine, Jacquard, Countess of Lovelace, Charles Babbage, Herman Hollerith.

and because the parts required could not be made well enough to work properly. Charles Babbage, if anyone, deserves to be called the father of the computer, but it was another hundred years before the ideas he had could be translated into reality, when the electronics industry began to put his ideas into practise.

Undoubtedly the biggest spur to the development of the computer came in the Second World War. Early British computers were used for weapons research and code-breaking. Even now many of the details of these machines are still secret. After the war the big companies began making computers for civilian use. In England the Lyons Electronic Office (LEO) was developed by a famous catering firm and in the USA, Sperry-Univac and IBM were among the first to start marketing the machines on a big scale.

Computer programming started with Ada, Countess of Lovelace and the daughter of the poet Byron. She was a friend of Charles Babbage and she developed programming ideas for his machines. Today she is honoured by having a computer language 'ADA' named after her.

Giants and Dwarfs

The first computers made after the war seemed like giants with tiny brains — in fact they can be regarded as dinosaurs of the computer age! They were very large and occupied a lot of space. They looked very complicated with racks of electronic components, thousands of valves and miles of cable. Famous early computers included ENIAC, EDVAC and UNIVAC. They used a lot of electricity and were prone to failure as valves burnt out. ENIAC contained 18,000 valves; imagine trying to find the one that had broken! These early computers made their appearance in the late 1940's. Together they are called *First Generation* computers.

In 1948 the transistor was invented and paved the way for miniaturisation. Transistors quickly replaced valves and in the home portable transistor radios quickly took the place of big valve 'wireless sets'. The same thing happened with computers. These machines are called 'Second Generation' computers.

The 'Third Generation' came with the introduction of the integrated circuit. These devices were made up of several transistors fabricated on the Silicon Chip. The space race of the 1960's was a great factor in speeding up their development.

In the 1970's the advent of microelectronics brought the 'Fourth Generation', as the Silicon Chip developed further. The USA and Japan are two countries in the forefront of this technology. In the 1980's, we are already talking of the 'Fifth Generation', but unlike the early generations this has more to do with development in computer programming than with electronics.

What do you say to a Computer?

What is a computer program?
What do they look like?
How do you write one?
Is it easy?

Before any computer can do a job it needs to be instructed on how to do it. The set of instructions is called a computer program.

The important thing to remember is that once set up to do a job the computer can repeat it indefinitely. Writing the computer program takes time and patience but it only has to be done once! However, great care needs to be taken to make a program that works well and does not contain any errors. More important, perhaps, is the need to get it to do the right job!

A computer programming language is just that — a LANGUAGE. It is a man-made language carefully designed and with a small vocabulary; but it is a language that you have to learn to write and read — though not yet speak! Because it has its own rules of grammar most people find that it takes some time to become an expert but almost everyone can write simple programs very quickly. The language that you are going to come across most frequently when using home computers is called BASIC.

BASIC means Beginners All-purpose Symbolic Instruction Code. It was designed in the USA by teachers who wanted an easy-to-learn language for their students. In recent years it has become very popular indeed.

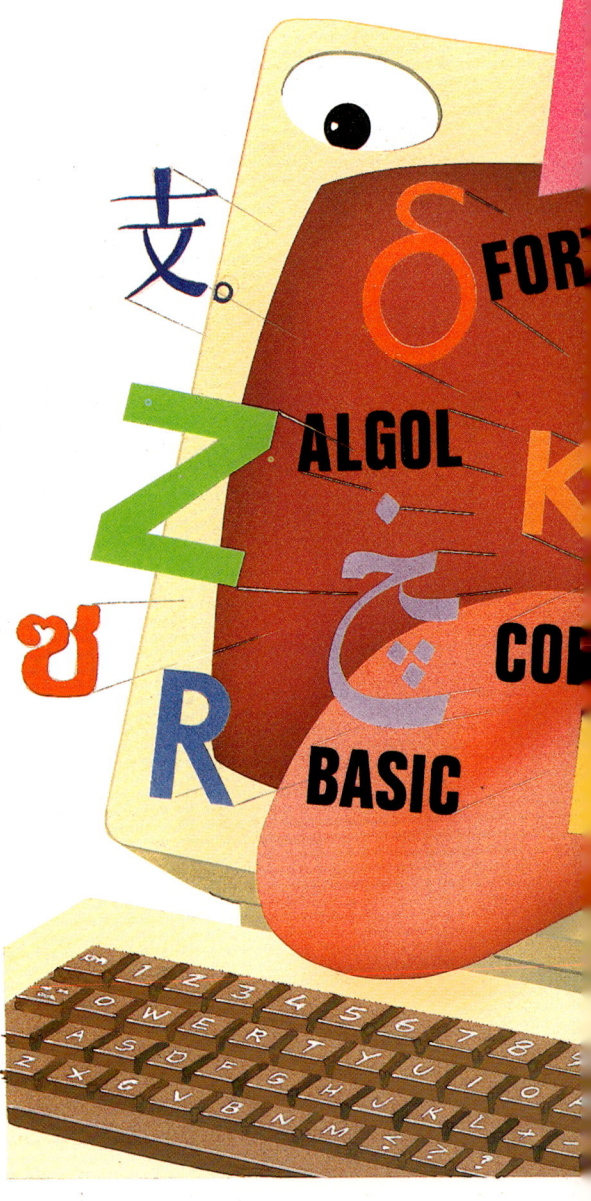

It is important to remember that there are many different languages and some are more useful than others for solving particular problems. COBOL (Common Business

since been invented because people thought that there ought to be more 'structured' languages. 'Structured' means that the language has features in it which:

1] Make it more likely that the program does exactly what the programmer intended.

2] Make it easily understood by someone other than the original programmer, when the program has to be changed for some reason. Such a language is ALGOL [Algorithmic Language]. Lots of these type of languages have been developed. A well-known example is PASCAL. This is popular in universities and colleges but it is only just finding its way onto the home computer market. There is always a search to find better and quicker methods of writing programs. We can expect new languages to be developed all the time. In the UK and USA the language ADA is becoming more popular.

With all these languages it is not surprising that it is possible to be an expert in one and a complete beginner in another! To make it more complicated there may be many dialects of the same language. Most of the languages mentioned follow international standards agreed by lots of countries. But even so a language like COBOL or BASIC will be different in detail when it is written for two different machines. As you can imagine this can be quite a headache if you try to run the same program on different machines and get different answers! Beware of this problem when copying programs from magazines. You may spend a long time typing a program which in the end doesn't work!

Orientated Language] is most widespread in commerce and industry. FORTRAN [Formula Translation] was developed as a scientific language.

More complicated languages have

Writing a program begins when you have a *reason* for using a computer. We call this reason a 'problem'. A computer program is a way of solving the problem.

You first need to 'analyse' the problem so that you understand exactly what will be required of the program. To analyse the problem means to examine it thoroughly and to describe in great detail all aspects of it.

For example: supposing a manager wants to pay his employees by computer he may state the problem in a very general way like this:

"I want to pay my staff by computer so that I will save time each week or month and so that I will know that their payslips are correct."

What a lot of questions are hidden! First how do you calculate pay? Well, two basic facts needed are the number of hours worked by the employee and how much an hour he is paid. Then, what about overtime or tax? Only when a complete understanding is reached could we set about writing the program.

Take another example. Supposing we want to write a games program:

"I want an exciting arcade game with space-ships and phasar guns, aliens and a rescue mission to the planet Mars."

The rules of the game have to be decided long before we start writing the program. How many aliens will there be? What numbers of points will we score for each alien space-ship destroyed? How many lives do we have? Will the game go faster as we get better?

It may come as a surprise to know that the description of what the program should do under all circumstances is often a very bulky document. It may take a lot longer to write than the program itself!

Wake Up!

How do you analyse a problem and ensure that there are no loose ends, no unforeseen conditions? One way is to draw a *flowchart*. As its name suggests a flowchart is a diagram which shows the flow through a program. They can be very complex and detailed but let's look at a simple example, getting up and going to school!

Alarm clock rings

weekend — YES — Stay in bed a bit longer

NO

Get dressed

NO

Hungry? — YES

Get breakfast

Eat breakfast

Get washed

Is Mum satisfied with washing? — NO

YES

Go to school

Is this flowchart the way you do it? Can it be improved at all? Note that questions are asked in the diamond shaped boxes. The questions are phrased so that the answer is either 'yes' of 'no'. The oblong boxes describe actions which are done and the arrows show the path or flow of the chart.

Try drawing flowcharts to show the following:
a] crossing the road
b] writing and posting a letter
c] putting up a tent
  Get your friends to test the charts to see if there are any mistakes!

17

Getting Started

You may not have a home computer yourself but it is quite likely that you will be able to use one belonging to a friendly neighbour or perhaps your school. If you get a chance try out some of the instructions on the following pages. They will help you to get used to computer language.

When you unpack a home computer you'll find it consists of the keyboard unit (in which the computer itself is usually located) and a number of cables to be attached to your TV set or monitor, the tape recorder and power supply.

Your manual will tell you exactly how to set it up but it will probably look something like this:

You must tune the TV to an unused channel or video station until the picture becomes sharp and clear and shows something like this:

**CBM BASIC V2
3583 BYTES FREE
READY**

Flashing Cursor

The initial display on a COMMODORE Vic 20

So far so good, but how do you get started? Type the letters N, E, W one after another. You will notice the cursor moves each time you press a key. The cursor points to the next position on the screen.

The cursor may be a square block like the Commodore example, or it may be a sign or perhaps an underlined character. Each machine is different.

After typing NEW; press the key marked ENTER. This key also has different names depending on the whim of the manufacturer. It could be called 'CARRIAGE RETURN' [CR], LINE FEED', 'NEWLINE' or may simply be a larger key than the others!

The effect of pressing ENTER is to display the READY prompt inviting you to type in the first line of the program.

After each line press the ENTER key. Have a practice with the following example.

```
10 INPUT A
20 INPUT B
30 LET C = A + B
40 PRINT C
```

Each line starts with a number. Then comes the computer instruction itself — the 'statement'. It usually consists of a verb [e.g.: INPUT] and a 'variable' name. Variables are the data items that the computer is dealing with. In BASIC variables can be numeric and refer only to a number or they can refer to letters, in which case they are called 'string variables'. Numeric variables are identified by single character names [e.g.: A, B, etc.]. String variables have names made up of a letter and a dollar sign [e.g.: A$].

INPUT is a BASIC verb meaning that the operator is to type in something, in this case a number to be called A. Line 20 asks the person using the program to type in a second number.

Line C adds the two numbers in A and B together. A and B, the variable names, actually refer to the parts of the computer's memory where the numbers typed in are stored.

The statement
LET C = A + B
really means:

"Add the number previously typed in and stored in A to the number which is stored in B, putting the answer in the storage position C."

PRINT C means 'display the answer'.

What happens when you've typed the first program? Nothing! The computer has stored your program in memory. It will do nothing [waiting with infinite patience] until you do something.

Type RUN and the computer will probably reply:

```
?
```

This means the program is working! Type in a number, say 50, and you should get another question mark in response.

```
?50
?
```

The computer is asking you to type in variable B. Type another number, say 40, and you will get the answer immediately.

```
?50
?40
90
```

The program has finished. Typing RUN again will cause it to be repeated so that you can type in different numbers.

NEW and RUN are BASIC commands. They tell the computer to do a specific job. Another useful command is LIST which will display your program statements. Commands work when typed. The lines in your program are statements and will only work when the program itself works.

Get it Right!

Let's learn BASIC! To do this you need a problem to solve. You could pick a complex and exciting video game but that might prove a bit difficult to start with. How about a simple quiz game for your first program?

It's a quiz with a difference — it's a spelling test!

What should it do? Here are some suggestions.
a) The person playing the game ought to know some instructions to explain the game.
b) The rules of the game will be that the computer will show the player a word and ask if it is the correct spelling. If the player thinks it is correct they reply with a Y. If they think it is wrong they reply N. If the player is right they score 10 points but if they are wrong they lose 5 points!
c) Bonus points can be scored if the player knows a word is spelled wrongly and can give the correct spelling.
d) The computer keeps a scorecard and will display the highest score if more than one player is involved in the game.

Now you are ready to type the program statements line by line. But before you do so type the word NEW first. This clears out any program you may already have in the memory.

A word or warning — refer to your computer manual FIRST. The SPELLING program uses only a small number of basic instructions and these should be portable between different machines. But given the great variety of microcomputers there is always a chance that you will need to make a slight change.

List of Variables
Numeric Variables
H High Score
S Current player's score
T Timing counter

String Variables
A$ Player's answer [Y or N]
C$ Correct spelling
E$ End
G$ Go
H$ Name of highest scoring player
N$ Name of current player
R$ Have another go [Y or N]
T$ Player's try at spelling word
W$ Word
Y$ Correct spelling indicator [Y or N]

The program begins with a REM statement. This is a note or remark to the reader of the program and does not actually form part of the program itself.

You will see that each statement begins with a line number. These are important for two reasons:
a) The line numbers determine the order in which the statements are obeyed by the computer.
b) If you want to jump from one statement to another the number of the second statement is referred to as a 'label'. It is written immediately following the GOTO verb. There are several examples in the SPELLING program.

A Computer Game Program to Help you Learn BASIC

This flowchart is a simple way of showing how the program will work, providing the programmer gets it right!

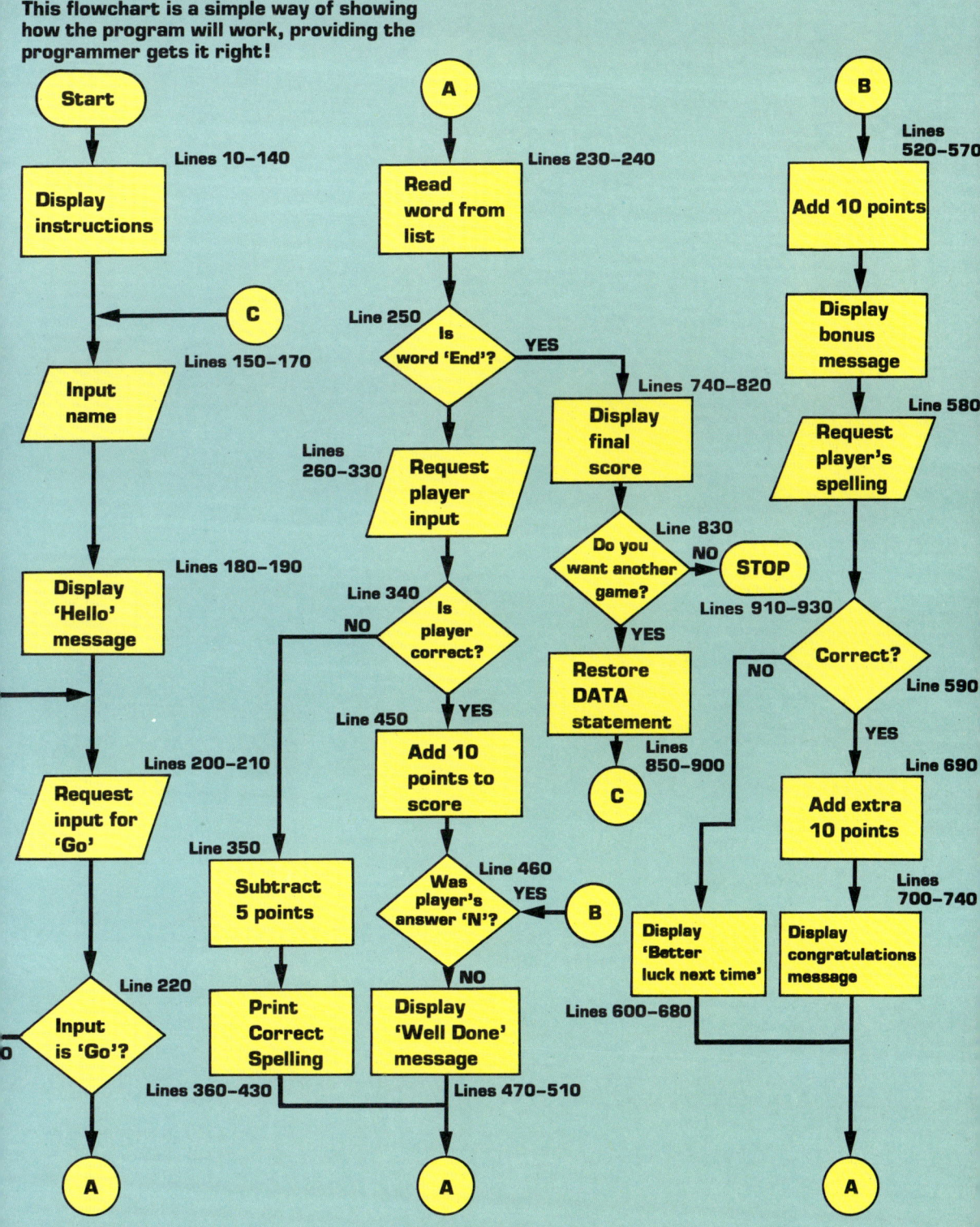

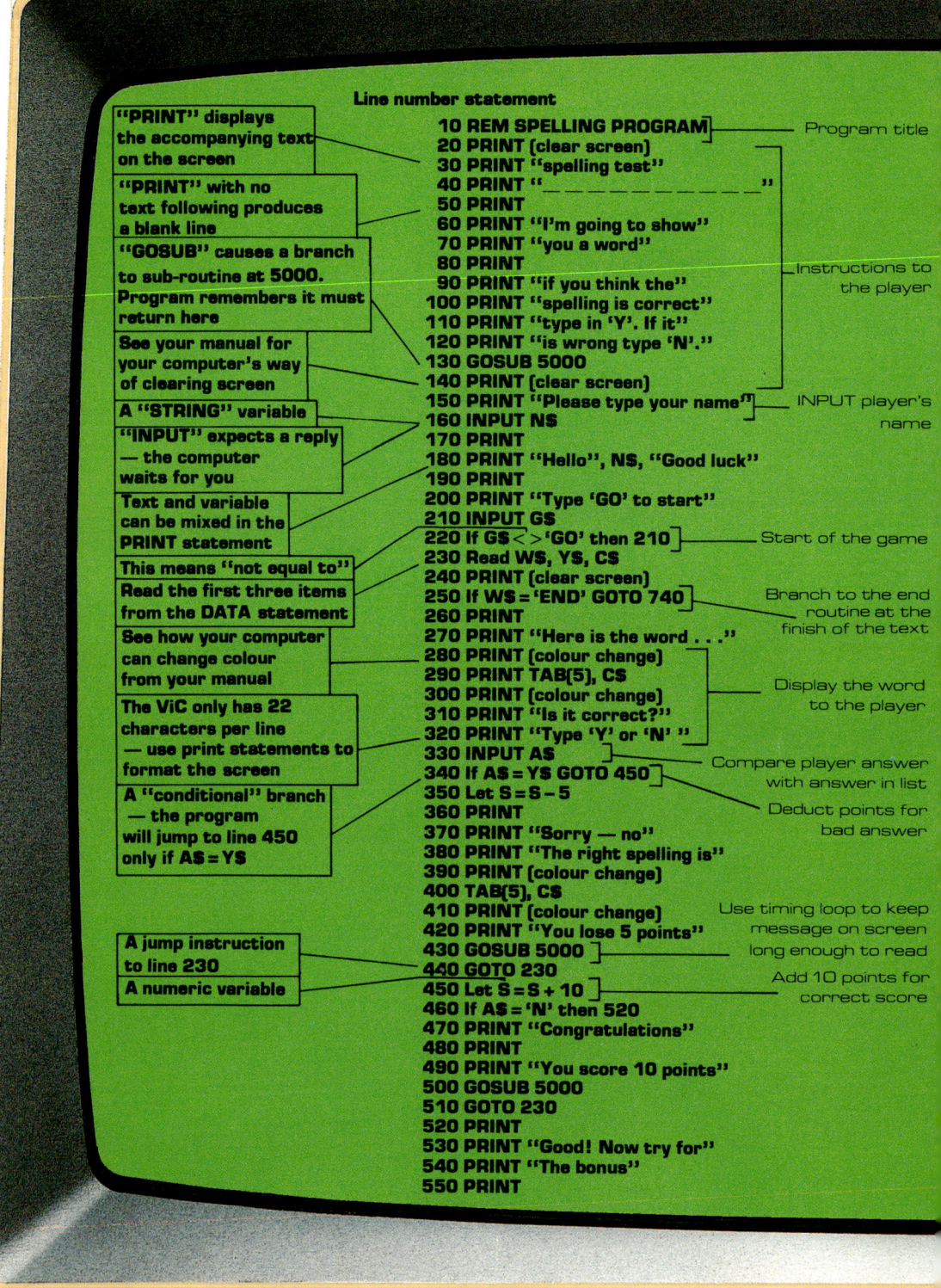

Line number statement

"PRINT" displays the accompanying text on the screen

"PRINT" with no text following produces a blank line

"GOSUB" causes a branch to sub-routine at 5000. Program remembers it must return here

See your manual for your computer's way of clearing screen

A "STRING" variable

"INPUT" expects a reply — the computer waits for you

Text and variable can be mixed in the PRINT statement

This means "not equal to"

Read the first three items from the DATA statement

See how your computer can change colour from your manual

The ViC only has 22 characters per line — use print statements to format the screen

A "conditional" branch — the program will jump to line 450 only if A$ = Y$

A jump instruction to line 230

A numeric variable

```
10 REM SPELLING PROGRAM
20 PRINT (clear screen)
30 PRINT "spelling test"
40 PRINT "_ _ _ _ _ _ _ _ _ _ _ _ "
50 PRINT
60 PRINT "I'm going to show"
70 PRINT "you a word"
80 PRINT
90 PRINT "if you think the"
100 PRINT "spelling is correct"
110 PRINT "type in 'Y'. If it"
120 PRINT "is wrong type 'N'."
130 GOSUB 5000
140 PRINT (clear screen)
150 PRINT "Please type your name"
160 INPUT N$
170 PRINT
180 PRINT "Hello", N$, "Good luck"
190 PRINT
200 PRINT "Type 'GO' to start"
210 INPUT G$
220 If G$ < > 'GO' then 210
230 Read W$, Y$, C$
240 PRINT (clear screen)
250 If W$ = 'END' GOTO 740
260 PRINT
270 PRINT "Here is the word . . ."
280 PRINT (colour change)
290 PRINT TAB(5), C$
300 PRINT (colour change)
310 PRINT "Is it correct?"
320 PRINT "Type 'Y' or 'N' "
330 INPUT A$
340 If A$ = Y$ GOTO 450
350 Let S = S – 5
360 PRINT
370 PRINT "Sorry — no"
380 PRINT "The right spelling is"
390 PRINT (colour change)
400 TAB(5), C$
410 PRINT (colour change)
420 PRINT "You lose 5 points"
430 GOSUB 5000
440 GOTO 230
450 Let S = S + 10
460 If A$ = 'N' then 520
470 PRINT "Congratulations"
480 PRINT
490 PRINT "You score 10 points"
500 GOSUB 5000
510 GOTO 230
520 PRINT
530 PRINT "Good! Now try for"
540 PRINT "The bonus"
550 PRINT
```

Program title

Instructions to the player

INPUT player's name

Start of the game

Branch to the end routine at the finish of the text

Display the word to the player

Compare player answer with answer in list

Deduct points for bad answer

Use timing loop to keep message on screen long enough to read

Add 10 points for correct score

The SPELLING program illustrates quite a few features of BASIC.
—How variables can be numeric or string.

—The use of the BASIC statements: LET, PRINT, TAB, GOTO, IF . . . . THEN, INPUT, DATA, READ, RESTORE, GOSUB, RETURN.

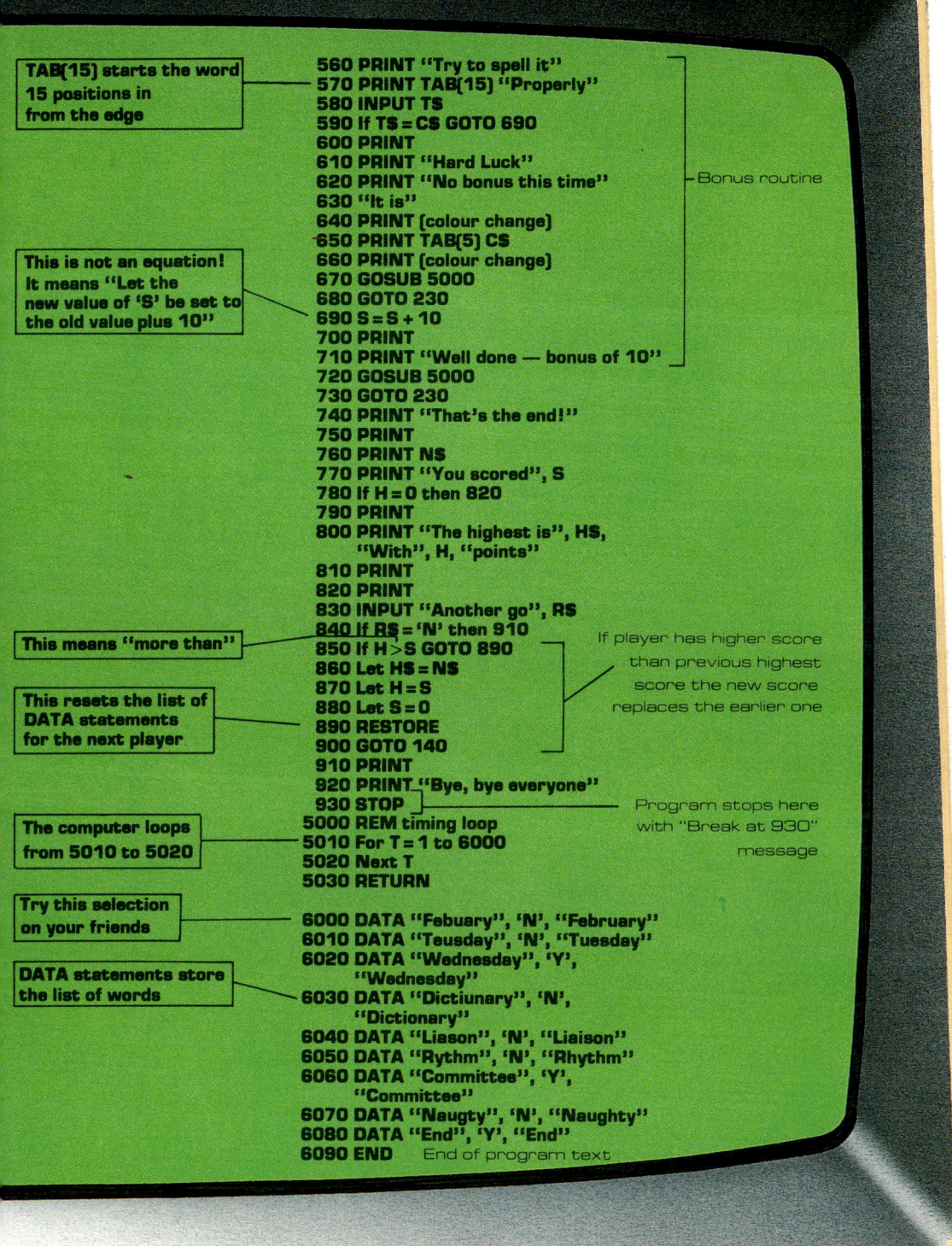

TAB(15) starts the word 15 positions in from the edge

This is not an equation! It means "Let the new value of 'S' be set to the old value plus 10"

This means "more than"

This resets the list of DATA statements for the next player.

The computer loops from 5010 to 5020

Try this selection on your friends

DATA statements store the list of words

```
560 PRINT "Try to spell it"
570 PRINT TAB(15) "Properly"
580 INPUT T$
590 If T$ = C$ GOTO 690
600 PRINT
610 PRINT "Hard Luck"
620 PRINT "No bonus this time"
630 "It is"
640 PRINT (colour change)
650 PRINT TAB(5) C$
660 PRINT (colour change)
670 GOSUB 5000
680 GOTO 230
690 S = S + 10
700 PRINT
710 PRINT "Well done — bonus of 10"
720 GOSUB 5000
730 GOTO 230
740 PRINT "That's the end!"
750 PRINT
760 PRINT N$
770 PRINT "You scored", S
780 If H = 0 then 820
790 PRINT
800 PRINT "The highest is", H$,
        "With", H, "points"
810 PRINT
820 PRINT
830 INPUT "Another go", R$
840 If R$ = 'N' then 910
850 If H > S GOTO 890
860 Let H$ = N$
870 Let H = S
880 Let S = 0
890 RESTORE
900 GOTO 140
910 PRINT
920 PRINT "Bye, bye everyone"
930 STOP
5000 REM timing loop
5010 For T = 1 to 6000
5020 Next T
5030 RETURN
6000 DATA "Febuary", 'N', "February"
6010 DATA "Teusday", 'N', "Tuesday"
6020 DATA "Wednesday", 'Y',
        "Wednesday"
6030 DATA "Dictiunary", 'N',
        "Dictionary"
6040 DATA "Liason", 'N', "Liaison"
6050 DATA "Rythm", 'N', "Rhythm"
6060 DATA "Committee", 'Y',
        "Committee"
6070 DATA "Naugty", 'N', "Naughty"
6080 DATA "End", 'Y', "End"
6090 END     End of program text
```

— Bonus routine

If player has higher score than previous highest score the new score replaces the earlier one

Program stops here with "Break at 930" message

—Arithmetic operations (e.g.: +, −)
—Changing the flow-branching using the GOTO statement.
—An example of a loop.

You can improve on the program using colour, sound and graphics — but this we leave to you!

Now You're Talking!

The binary code is the basis of computer language. To understand how a computer works you must have some knowledge of *Binary Arithmetic*.

Why is the binary system so important for computers? The answer is simple. At the heart of the computer are the CHIPS. On the CHIPS are the thousands of electronic circuits carrying electrical signals or pulses.

A pulse is, as its name suggests, 'on' or 'off'. An early example of a binary code is the Morse Code. This uses 'dots' and 'dashes' when it is written down and if you ever hear Morse Code you'll recognise the dash as a longer sound than the dot.

The word 'binary' really means 'two'. A code like the Morse Code which uses only two symbols is a binary code. Something like a light switch which only has two positions: 'on' and 'off', is a binary device.

An electrical pulse can be used to represent '1' which also means 'on'. The absence of a pulse is '0' or 'off'. The 'zero' signal or no-pulse is as important as the pulse or 'one' pulse.

How do you do arithmetic using only the symbols 1 and 0?

It looks strange but it follows the same rules as ordinary arithmetic. In ordinary decimal arithmetic we use ten different symbols. We use the numerals 0, 1, 2, 3, 4, 5, 6, 7, 8 and 9. We combine these numerals and write for example:

'500' meaning 'five hundred'
or
'29' meaning 'twenty nine'.

Actually '29' is really shorthand for saying:

two tens plus nine units.

If we write '333', meaning three hundred and thirty three, we have used the same symbol [3] but its value has been multiplied by 10 each time we move one place to the left. It really means:

three hundred	**(3 × 10 × 10)**
plus	
thirty	**(3 × 10)**
plus	
three	**(3)**

In binary arithmetic the symbols are multiplied by 2 for each position we move to the left. Inside the computer complex calculations are reduced to arithmetic done in noughts and ones!

Here are some binary numbers with their decimal equivalents:

Binary		**Decimal**
1	equivalent to	1
10		1 × 2 = 2
100		1 × 2 × 2 = 4
1000		1 × 2 × 2 × 2 = 8
11		1 × 2 plus 1 = 3
101		1 × 2 × 2 plus 1 = 5
111		1 × 2 × 2 plus 1 × 2 plus 1 = 7

Got that? Read it over carefully to make sure you understand the principle of binary numbers. The next few sums are examples of simple arithmetic using the Rules of Binary Addition.

RULES FOR ADDITION

0 + 0 = 0
0 + 1 = 1
1 + 0 = 1
1 + 1 = 10

EXAMPLES:

Binary	Decimal
10	2
+ 1	+ 1
11	3

Binary	Decimal
101	5
+ 10	+ 2
111	7

Binary	Decimal
101	5
+ 1	+ 1
110	6
1	

carry one

Binary	Decimal
11	3
+ 1	+ 1
100	4
11	

carry carry

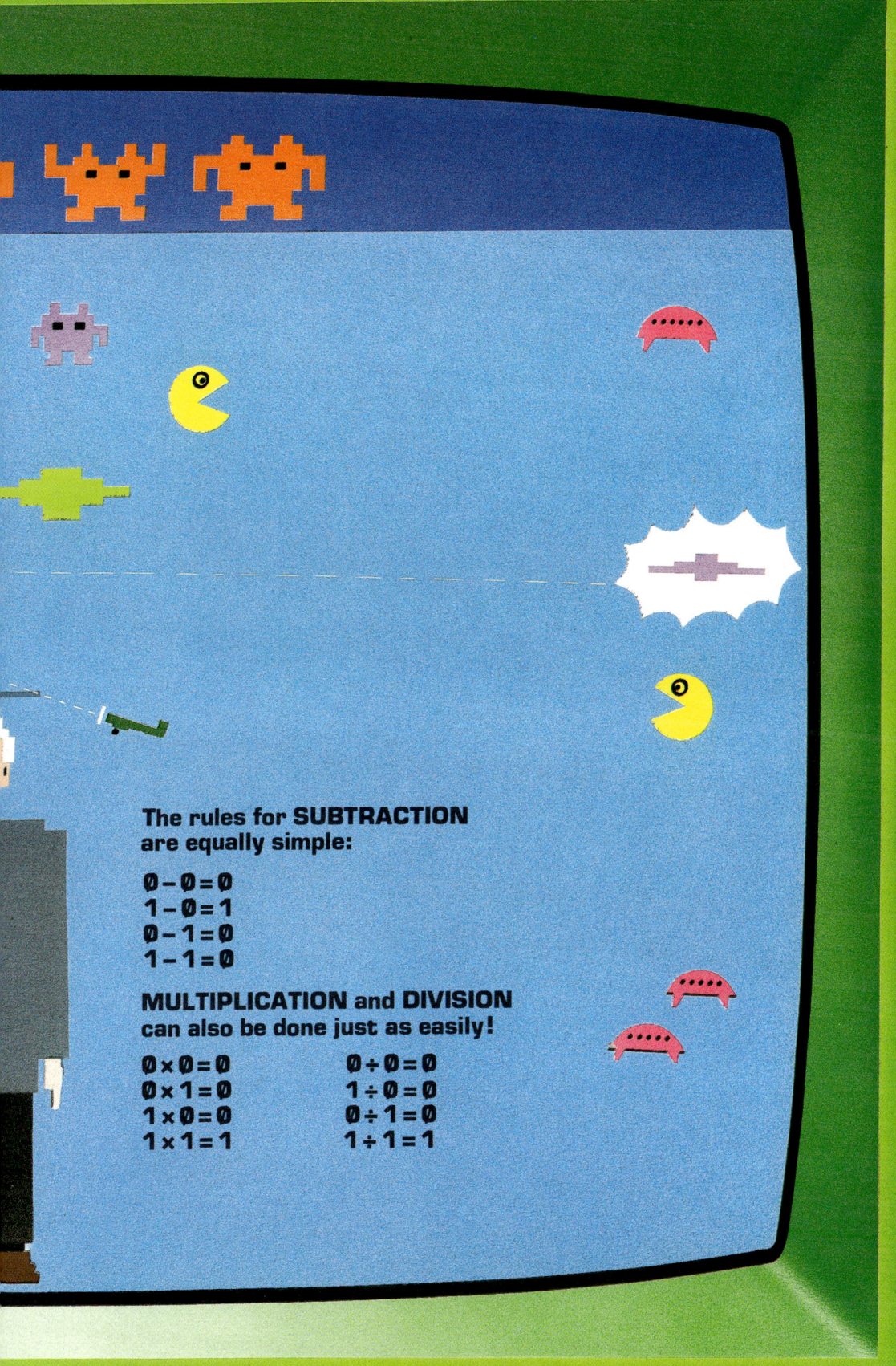

The rules for **SUBTRACTION**
are equally simple:

$0 - 0 = 0$
$1 - 0 = 1$
$0 - 1 = 0$
$1 - 1 = 0$

MULTIPLICATION and **DIVISION**
can also be done just as easily!

$0 \times 0 = 0$ $0 \div 0 = 0$
$0 \times 1 = 0$ $1 \div 0 = 0$
$1 \times 0 = 0$ $0 \div 1 = 0$
$1 \times 1 = 1$ $1 \div 1 = 1$

Computer Words

Apart from its use for arithmetic the binary code is also used to translate words. Computer programs are translated into binary code before they can be used.

Computers are often described in terms of the 'word length'. You will hear people talk about '8-bit' or '16-bit' computers, for example. This has nothing to do with their memory size. Instead it refers to the number of binary digits [BITS] that can be transferred between the different parts of the CPU at any one time.

The word length is an important determining feature of a computer. It defines how large or small a range for numbers can be dealt with in the machine and it also limits the range of codes that can be used. A very common grouping is to use 8 bits, which is often referred to as a BYTE.

Imagine a four-bit computer. Here is the complete range of binary digits that can be coded in 4 bits:

Binary	Decimal
0000	0
0001	1
0010	2
0011	3
0100	4
0101	5
0110	6
0111	7
1000	8
1001	9
1010	10
1011	11
1100	12
1101	13
1110	14
1111	15

The four-bit computer can handle arithmetic so long as the answer is not more than 15!

```
 Ø11Ø                6
+                   +
 Ø111                7
 ————               ——
 11Ø1               13
 ————               ——
But
 1ØØ1                9
+                   +
 Ø111                7
 ————               ——
BANG!               16
 ————               ——
```

Computer designers overcome the problem by using a longer word length (16, 32 and 48 are common) and by combining words together when dealing with very large (or very small) numbers.

An alternative explanation of our four-bit codes would be to regard each combination as a letter:

```
ØØØØ        A
ØØØ         B
ØØ1Ø        C
ØØ11        D
Ø1ØØ        E
Ø1Ø1        F
Ø11Ø        G
Ø111        H
1ØØØ        I
1ØØ1        J
1Ø1Ø        K
1Ø11        L
11ØØ        M
11Ø1        N
111Ø        O
1111        P
```

What about the letters 'Q' to 'Z'? This is another case where there aren't enough codes to go round!

In an 8-bit BYTE there are 256 different codes, from ØØØØØØØØ to 11111111! There are more than enough codes for:—
Twenty six capital letters of the alphabet (A–Z)
The alphabet in small letters (a–z)
Currency signs like £ and $
Special letters like ones with accents in certain languages
Special symbols such as & and ?

If it was left up to the individual designers of computers no doubt they would all have decided to use different coding systems. Luckily, however, most conform to standard coding systems that have developed in recent years.

What's Going on in There?

What happens to the program inside the computer? How are the words and numbers we write in BASIC actually made to work? This is a complicated process, so go through it slowly, and reread it if you don't understand the first time. It might help if you then go through it with someone who already understands computers so that they can help you out on the tricky bits. However, once you understand you'll find it quite simple!

The program and the data are stored in the computer's memory in the form of binary codes. We have looked at some ways in which letters and numbers can be represented as a string of binary digits or bits. We saw how several bits are grouped together into bytes.

The translation from a form that you and I can read and write into the computer's internal code is done in several ways.

Typically BASIC is 'interpreted' line by line. That means that when you type the RUN command, which means 'Carry out this program', each line of BASIC is translated one after another. This translation is done every time the program is used.

An alternative method is to translate the program once and store the translated version. This is often called COMPILATION and programs written in languages like COBOL or FORTRAN are nearly always compiled rather than interpreted.

Remember that computers are made up of electronic circuits. A silicon chip is composed of thousands of circuits but imagine a simple electrical circuit such as you would find in a torch.

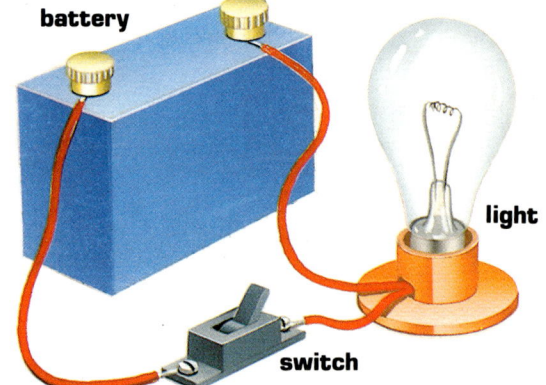

An electrical engineer uses special circuit diagrams to describe the picture.

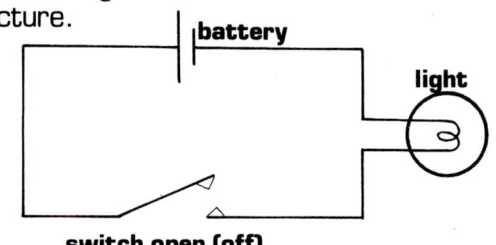

switch open (off)

Obviously the light only comes on when the switch is ON. But what happens if you have two switches in the circuit?

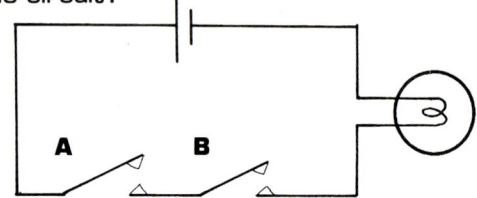

If switch A is ON but switch B is OFF the light won't shine because there is still not a continuous path for the elctrical current to flow through.

You can work out all the combinations of what might happen and put them in a TRUTH TABLE.

INPUT		OUTPUT
Switch A	Switch B	Light
ON	ON	SHINES
ON	OFF	OFF
OFF	ON	OFF
OFF	OFF	OFF

The light only shines when switch A and B are both on.

This TRUTH TABLE shows the operation of a computer AND gate. In a computer circuit a 'gate' is a device that sends out a given signal depending upon what is put in.

If you replace the switches in a simple circuit by a pair arranged in a different pattern this is what you get:

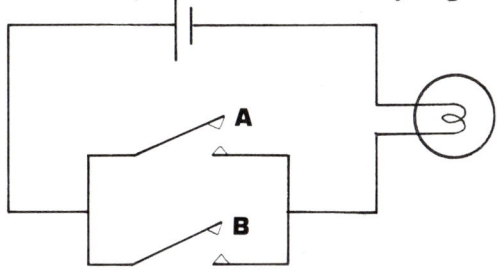

If one switch is closed but the other one is open you will still get the light to shine because there is still a continuous path for the electricity to flow through. The light only stops shining when both switches are off.

You can draw another TRUTH TABLE:

INPUT		OUTPUT
Switch A	Switch B	Lamp
ON	ON	SHINES
ON	OFF	SHINES
OFF	ON	SHINES
OFF	OFF	OFF

In this table the light shines if either switch A or switch B is on. The TRUTH TABLE describes the operation of a computer OR gate.

Computer scientists draw a symbol for each of these gates.

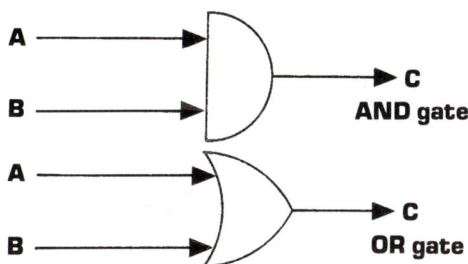

The TRUTH TABLES can be redrawn using 0's and 1's to represent the OFF and ON conditions:

AND gate				OR gate		
A	B	C		A	B	C
0	0	0		0	0	0
0	1	0		0	1	1
1	0	0		1	0	1
1	1	1		1	1	1

Compare the TRUTH TABLES against the rules for binary arithmetic. You will see that the tables are very similar.

There is a third type of gate, the NOT gate or 'inverter'. What this does is make the output opposite to what goes in.

The TRUTH TABLE for the NOT gate is very simple.

INPUT	CARRY
A 0 1 A	B 1 0 B

The NOT symbol.

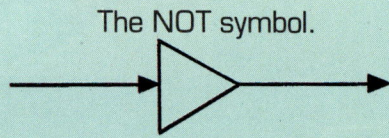

Let's now look at the BASIC instruction:

Line No	Instruction
10	Let X = 2 + 3

You want to add 2 and 3 and call the answer (which is 5) by the symbol X. When the decimal numbers 2 and 3 have been converted to binary numbers the sum looks like this:

Binary	Decimal
10	2
+ 11	+ 3
101	5

The rule for the binary addition can be expressed in a TRUTH TABLE.

INPUT A B	ANSWER C	CARRY
0 0	0	0
0 1	1	0
1 0	1	0
1 1	0	1

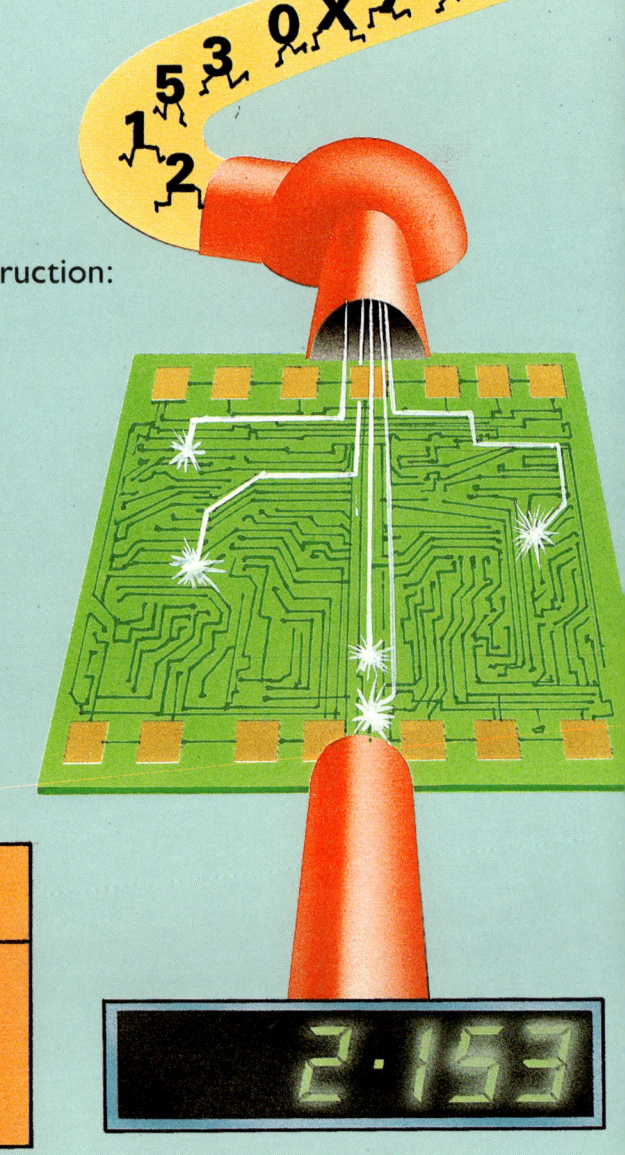

Here is the circuit to add the numbers together. It's called the 'HALF-ADDER' because the numbers being added together are only from one column of the sum at a time.

HOW DOES IT WORK?
Take one column from the sum.

The imputs to the first AND gate are 1 and Ø. Referring to the TRUTH TABLE for an AND gate you see that the output will be a Ø.

At point X on the diagram the no-pulse or zero pulse is put out by the AND gate. That zero signal goes out

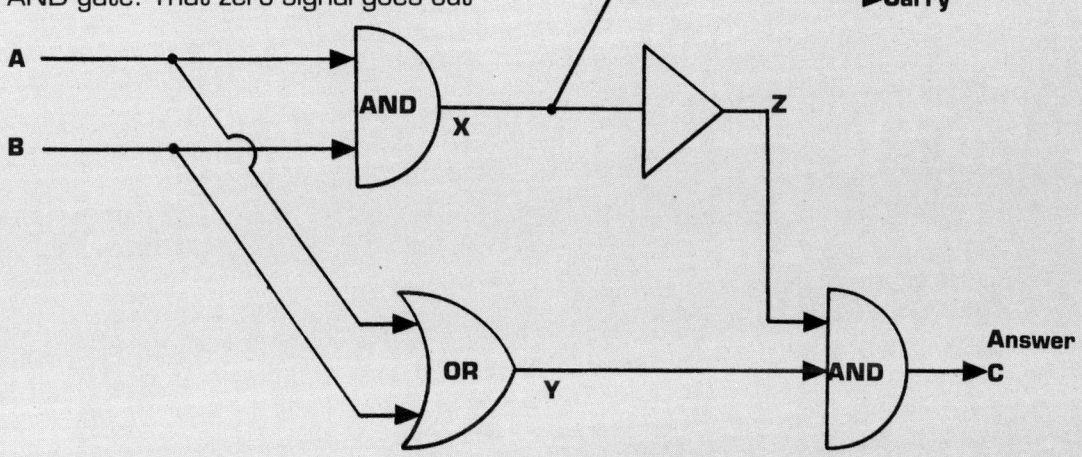

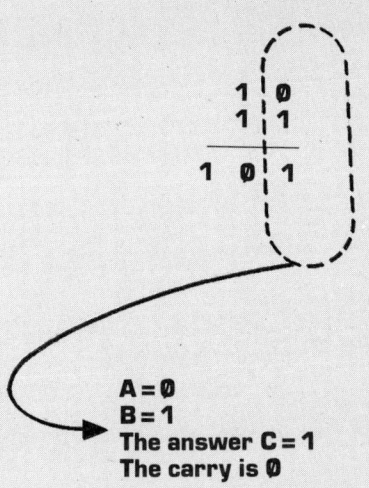

A = Ø
B = 1
The answer C = 1
The carry is Ø

on the carry line as a zero and also into the inverter, the NOT gate. The NOT gate makes its output opposite to its input so that at point Z there is a 1 signal.

Meanwhile the original A and B signals have been fed into the OR gate. From the TRUTH TABLE for an OR gate you know that in this instance the output at Y will be a 1 signal.

This 1 signal, together with the 1 signal from the NOT gate is fed into the second AND gate which produces the answer signal at C, which is going to be a 1!

You can see why it's called a HALF-ADDER. To add the 'carry' signal into the second column another HALF-ADDER will be required.

Even Computers Have Hearts!

The power and the versatile nature of the computer comes from the fact that it can do an enormous amount of work, calculating, sorting, storing and retrieving information. Computers do this automatically and at great speed. That's what makes them so useful to us.

It is a combination of hardware, bits actually built on to the computer, and software, things like programs, that make the computer what it is. The place where they come together at the very heart of the computer is called the CPU or CENTRAL PROCESSING UNIT.

What does it do? How does it do it?

We know that numbers and letters — the raw material for computer processing — are stored as binary codes in the computer. We have seen how logic circuits can deal with streams of data. The programs too are translated into binary patterns from the form that you and I can read.

What we now need is a controller to pull it all together — the CONTROL UNIT. The control unit is a bit like the conductor of an orchestra. Everyone is following the same program or plan (the musical score) but everyone is co-ordinated by the conductor.

The conductor may need a clock or a metronome if he isn't sure of the pace and this clock needs to be pretty accurate.

In the computer's CPU there is a special circuit producing a regular pulse at a specific interval. This is the timer or clock and is used to keep all the different parts of the machine working at the same pace.

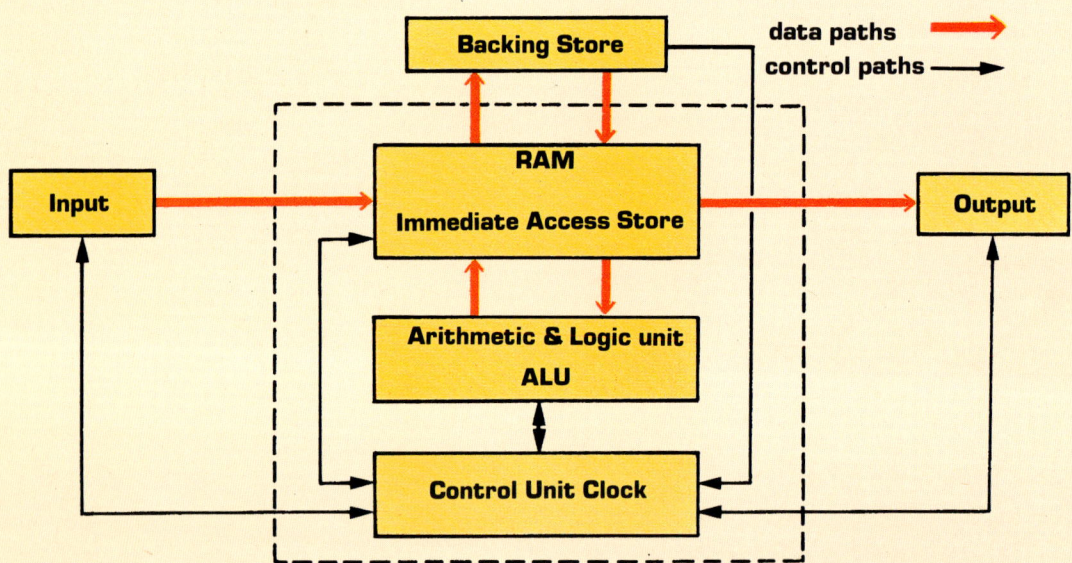

In the diagram there are two types of circuits — data paths for carrying information, and control paths which carry control signals from the control unit to the other components of the machine.

Data is sent from the input unit to the RAM immediate access store. From there it goes to the main backing store or to the ALU for processing before it goes to the output for display or printing.

You can imagine the data paths to be a road system with traffic lights at each junction. The control unit is sending a signal to turn the lights from red to green and so allow traffic paths to cross, stop, start or merge with each other.

Within the RAM data is stored at individual locations called 'addresses'. Imagine that you live in a block of flats; the postman knows where you can be located by your address. The variable names in BASIC are actually shorthand ways of describing locations in RAM, where the values of the variables are to be stored.

An example:

To the computer the basic instruction:

LET C = A + B

is too complex to work without further translation. After interpreting it might look more like this:

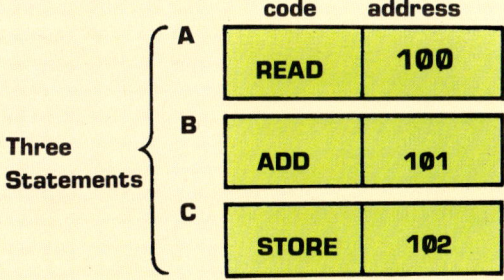

Even these would actually be in the form of a binary pattern but they mean:

a) "Read the number stored in location 100 into a special part of the ALU called the Accumulator."

b) "Add the number stored in location 101 to the contents of the accumulator. The answer is put back into the accumulator."

c) "Store the contents of the accumulator in location 102."

To carry out the first of the three statements the control unit has to go through several steps:

a) FETCH the first instruction from the memory. We know that this is in location 3. The controller has to use another special register to hold the 'address of the next instruction'. When a programmer uses a GOTO statement that alters the natural flow of the program by changing the value in the register.

b) DECODE the instruction — which means recognising it as 'READ' and place the address of the location to be addressed (i.e. 100) in yet another special register.

c) CARRY OUT the instruction, by going to the address specified in step b and actually retrieving the data from location 100, putting it into the accumulator.

This three-step process is carried out on regular beats of the clock, called CYCLES. When one instruction is finished the next instruction, the ADD instruction, can be fetched, decoded and executed and then finally, in our example, the STORE instruction is worked through. Only when this has been done has the computer finished

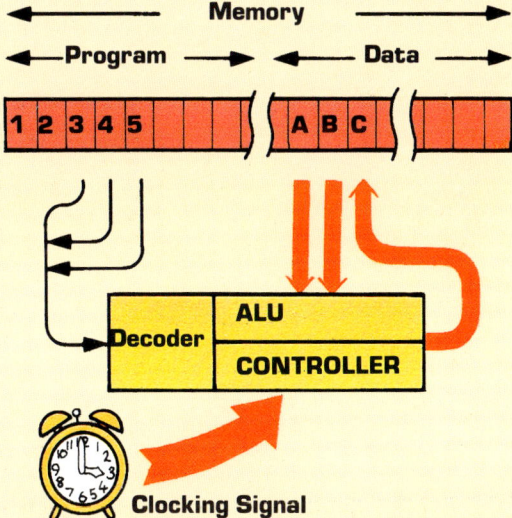

Clocking Signal

with the original BASIC statement. What a lot of work is going on behind the scenes! It's no wonder that the internal speeds of operation have to be so fast!

The Memory Machine

By now you should already know about RAM and ROM. These are immediate access memories within the CPU. Sometimes you can change the ROM and plug in a new cartridge (in games machines for example). What you are doing is changing the program, which to save space in the RAM has been put into a special memory chip instead.

You will almost certainly find that a home computer comes with a cassette tape recorder and sometimes a discette drive and some floppy discettes.

These devices are examples of what is called backing store. They are used for bulk storage of programs or data when not immediately required for use. Big computers use both magnetic tape and large capacity discs.

HOW A TAPE DRIVE WORKS

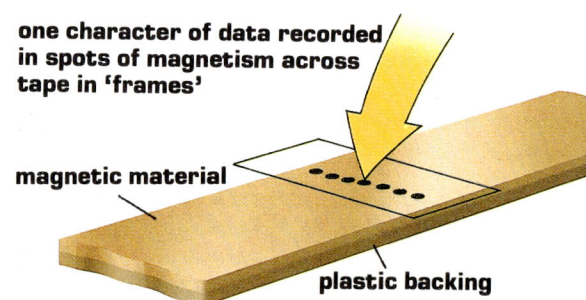

one character of data recorded in spots of magnetism across tape in 'frames'

magnetic material

plastic backing

About 60,000 characters can be stored per metre and tape reels can hold anything up to 700 metres of tape.

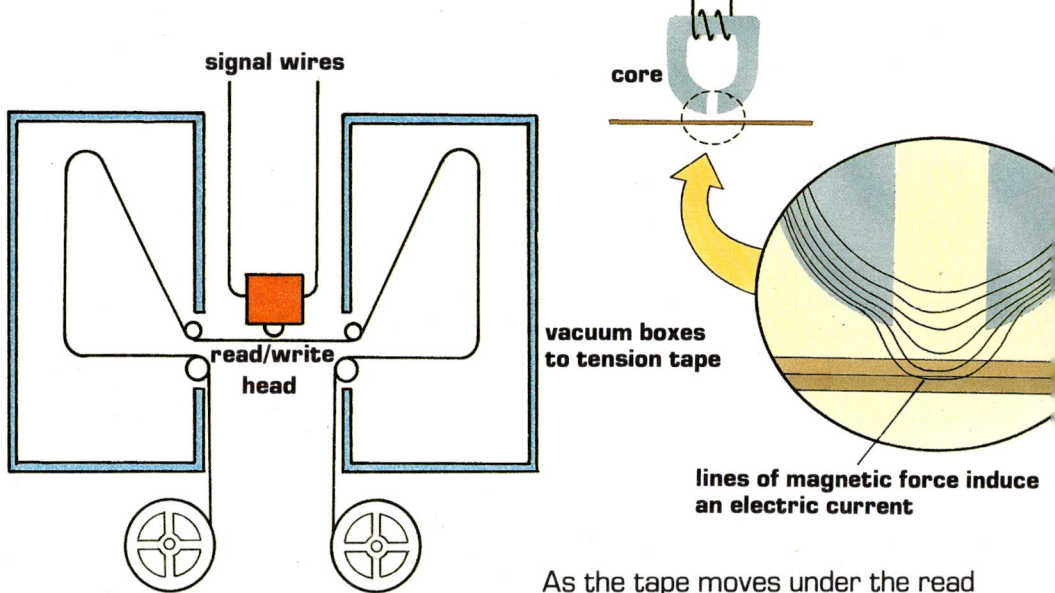

signal wires

read/write head

tape   reels

coil

core

vacuum boxes to tension tape

lines of magnetic force induce an electric current

As the tape moves under the read heads the patterns of magnetic force in the tape are detected and an electric current is induced in a coil. For writing the process is reversed.

Magnetic tapes are 'serial' devices — you must read from the start of the tape to the end to find something. Too bad if what you want is right at the end! On your cassette tapes, which use the same principles, you can overcome some of the delay by using very short tapes — but you'll need a lot of them!

HOW A DISC DRIVE WORKS

The disc revolves very fast and information passes under the read/write head. The information is recorded around each track. As much information is on the inner track as the outer track, although more compressed. The read/write head moves across the disc to read a specific track. The read/write head can jump backwards and forwards so information can be retrieved as and when it is required.

A disc pack is several discs mounted on a central spindle with a series of read/write heads in the form of a comb.

Disc capacities vary enormously — most large computers would use discs holding about 200 million characters. On some large computers disc packs are exchangeable — the operator can take them on and off — this gives almost limitless backing storage.

On a home computer you would probably be using floppy discs or discettes. These are much smaller, often only about 14 cm. in diameter, and consequently hold a lot less information — about 375,000 characters. However, larger capacity discettes with space for 1 or 2 million characters are becoming available.

Floppies are floppy because they are made of plastic, not brass or alloy like the big discs. They should not be mistreated. Don't bend them or crease them. Avoid high temperatures (such as a radiator) and spilling drinks over them! Remember also that they wear out. Unlike the big discs where the reading heads are a minute distance away from the surface, the read head on a floppy rubs against the surface all the time.

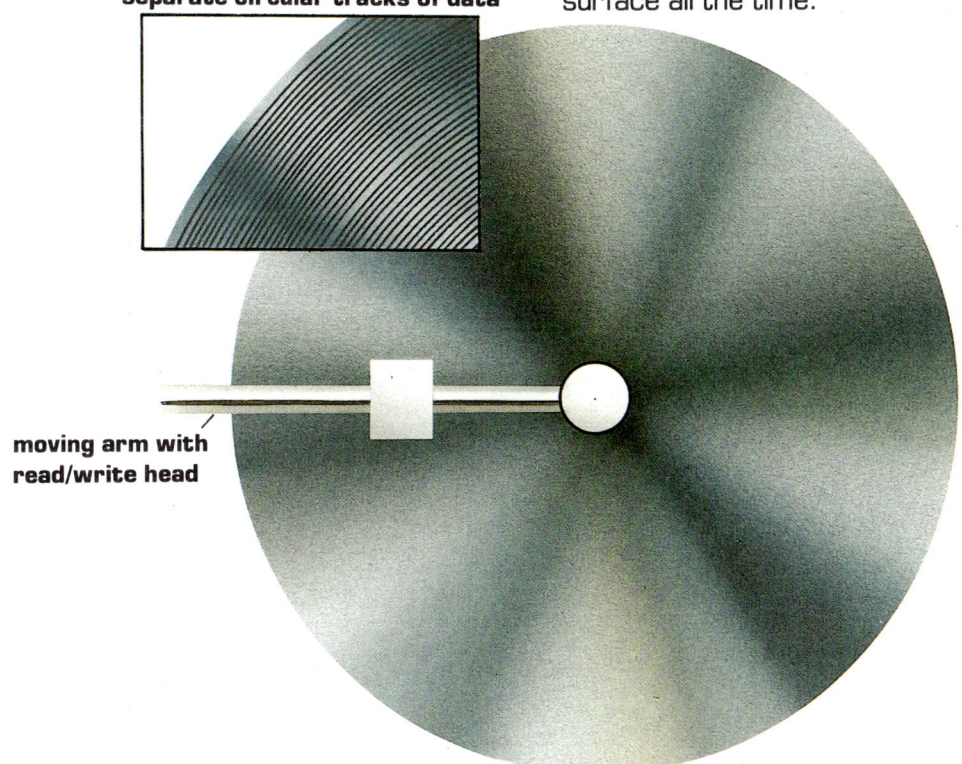

separate circular tracks of data

moving arm with read/write head

Getting the Message Out

The Central Processing Unit is important but even though it works at great speed for much of the time it is doing nothing at all. The reason is that it is waiting for information to come in or waiting to send processed data back to the world outside.

INPUT and OUTPUT devices are the things that slow a computer down. If you have ever typed even a short program into a home computer you will realise that input is a very slow process indeed! If only you could talk to it and dictate a program . . .

Well, you can't . . . yet! But experiments are under way and in time we will be able to do this. But by then, of course, we will want to think and pass our thoughts directly to the computer . . .

The most obvious method of input and output is the combined keyboard/screen unit. Most home computers house the keyboard and the CPU in the same box. If you use a domestic television as your screen that is normally the only output unit you have.

However, within these limits you can have a small loudspeaker (often used to make explosion noises to enhance games programs or to turn a home computer into a mini electronic organ). Joysticks and paddles are also useful features which allow more realistic input for games programs, rather than keys or a keyboard.

The MOUSE is a new input device which is quite popular at the moment. A MOUSE is a small hand-held device. As the operator rolls it across a flat surface left or right, towards him or away, a cursor on the screen is moved in the same direction.

Computers in business, however, generate a lot of paper and the most frequently used output mechanism is still a printer.

The LINE PRINTER, as its name suggests, prints a whole line of text at one time, often 132 or 160 characters per line, at speeds of up to 2000 and 3000 lines per minute.

Line printers mostly operate by moving a print hammer against an inked ribbon and then against the paper, very much like an ordinary type-writer. However, the letter-shapes are not embossed on the individual hammers; they are mounted on a print chain. Usually several sets of the complete alphabet are on the chain. The chain goes very rapidly across the paper and as the right letter comes under the hammer it is activated to print the character. Often chain printers print all of the same letters, say the 'e's', then a different letter.

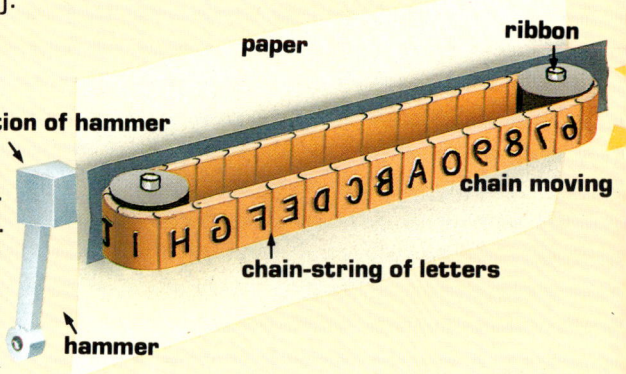

paper ribbon
motion of hammer
chain moving
chain-string of letters
hammer

DOT MATRIX printers are also used but these give slower speeds — perhaps 120-150 characters per second. Here the printing head consists of a set of fine pointed heads arranged in a rectangular pattern.

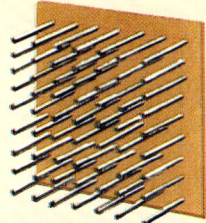

The shape of the letter is made up by activating certain pins which then punch against the inked ribbon and paper. Having printed one character the whole print head moves to the next position for the next character.

Specialised input/output devices are becoming very common. Bar-coding techniques have developed and it is now possible for a till to recognise the product you have just bought at a supermarket check-out, by passing the item across a special device which 'reads' the bar codes on the label.

Automatically the computer ensures that your check-out ticket shows the correct item and price. It probably relays your purchase to the supermarket's record of stocks so that the item can be reordered.

TELECOMMUNICATIONS
Computers do not need to be near to their source of input and can just as easily receive or transmit information to remote devices as they can to VDUs nearby.

Computer data can be sent over ordinary telephone wires by attaching special boxes at each end of the telephone link. These boxes convert the computer signals — the binary form — to that required for the telephone wire and vice versa.

Robot Power

In manufacturing industry all departments of a company are likely to use the computer extensively in one way or another.

Let's say that an order is received from a customer by the sales department. Using a VDU a sales clerk can find out if the required goods are in stock in the warehouse. If they are they can be reserved for the customer immediately using the computer. If there aren't enough items in stock the computer may be able to provide an estimate of how long the delay will be.

In the warehouse, the staff have a print-out of the order, produced on a printer in the warehouse. They may even be told the position of the goods within the warehouse by the computer. In some highly mechanised warehouses cranes, lifts and trolleys may be automatically sent by the computer to find the items.

When the goods have been selected for despatch the main computer is notified and the records of stock in the warehouse are updated. After despatch the customer's account will be updated to show the new amount standing. The delivery vehicle's route may also be decided by a computer! When the customer has received and paid for the goods the computer files are updated again.

In the accounts department all the financial threads are brought together; new sales are recorded, new orders to suppliers, the costs of production, labour and the value of items being made or sitting in the warehouse. This is useful information which helps the managers run the business efficiently. The computer's real worth is to record the flow of information and to cross-reference or analyse it very quickly.

DESIGNED BY COMPUTER

In the design department, especially in the aerospace, engineering and defence industries COMPUTER-AIDED DESIGN is a growing computer function.

'CAD' helps the design engineer to try out various solutions to a problem before settling on the best.

In general CAD machines are rather like electronic draught boards. The designer uses the screen to draw a picture using both a lightpen and a keyboard to input the information. Once the design is stored in the computer small changes, such as changing the size of a component, can be introduced and a revised drawing done almost immediately. Re-drawing by hand would take days or weeks for complex pieces of equipment.

CAD often includes facilities for working out the complicated calculations required of a design engineer, and makes his job a little easier!

ROBOT POWER

In manufacturing industry the robots aren't metallic creatures shaped like humans with flashing lights on their heads! They look much less interesting and they often don't move very far either!

A typical industrial robot will perform a small number of tasks in a set order in a set time. They have been programmed to do this small range of duties and nothing else. They're specialised computers — that's all!

A robot welder on a car assembly line may perform several welding operations on the car chassis. As the car passes slowly along the line the welding arm must move slightly. Having completed one weld the machine will move the arm to the next position. It may be that the arm has a 'wrist' attached to it so that the welding tool may be moved quite a lot to get at difficult spots. These robots will do the jobs with predictable precision and quality but if the shape of the car changes they have to be reprogrammed.

Put Your Money in Computers!

Banking involves the movement of money between individuals or companies and flows of money must be strictly controlled and measured. What better way to do this than the honest computer!

To most of us the most common form of banking is the ordinary cheque. Cheque processing is a fundamental banking operation and one for which computers are very widely used. About six million cheques a day are processed in the UK.

A cheque is an instruction by the person writing the cheque to his bank, telling them to pay a certain amount to another person. The person receiving the cheque pays into his own bank. Already on the cheque the account number, branch code and cheque number appear. These characters are printed in special magnetisable ink. When the cheque goes through the cheque-reading equipment the letters and numbers can be identified by the amount of electricity induced in the reading head by each character.

In London all the cheques are received at the Bankers Automated Clearing House (BACS), which sorts out who owes what to whom and sends off magnetic tapes containing the data to the major banks.

On a less complex level, banks are using computers as cash-dispensers and terminals which give the customer information about his account as well as handing out money. This comes in very useful when the banks themselves are closed!

The world of high finance

There are two areas of the finance industry which show the different ways in which computers can be used. In our society we use money as a way of measuring the value of something ["How much does it cost?"]. But we can also treat it as a commodity to be bought and sold in its own right. If you borrow money you don't get it for free; you have to pay a charge, 'interest', for it. If you are lending you expect to be paid interest.

Overnight lending

At the end of the working day a company can lend money overnight, for example to a borrower the other side of the world who needs to use it during their working day. The two companies don't usually deal with each other directly but go through the major international banks who act as middlemen. The computer is used to record the transaction and the interest rate prevailing at the instant that the loan is made. Subsequently the computers are used to track the loan and do the follow-up accounting.

A second area of use is in consumer finance. Here a financial company provides money to the householder — perhaps to enable him to buy a car or have an extension built onto a house. The loan is paid for by the consumer over a number of years, usually by monthly payments.

The lending company uses computers for a number of tasks. The credit-worthiness of the person wanting the loan is checked by reference to computer-held lists of people who might be bad credit risks. Then, when the loan is made, the lending company will use its own computer to note the receipt of each installment and keep track of the loan until it is paid off.

Insurance

In the insurance industry computers are used to ensure that insurance policies are kept up-to-date, that premiums are paid on time and that claims are paid when due. Insurance companies might decide that the items they have insured are so valuable that they would be wise to pass on, or 'cede' some of the risk. They decide to reinsure with additional insurers, called underwriters.

In London the centre for re-insurance is at LLOYDS. Individual Lloyds underwriters accept a small fraction of each risk. A Lloyds broker's job is to find an underwriter willing to accept a part of the risk, to collect the charge for insurance [the Premium] from his client and to split it amongst the individual underwriters. When a claim is made — perhaps as the result of an accident to a ship, for example, the broker's job is to collect the claims money from the underwriter and pass it back to the ceding company. The brokers use computers to do accounting and keep track of whether premiums have been received.

Look, No Driver!

It's not quite as drastic as the title suggests but computers increasingly work in the field of travel and transport.

Air

In the air computers are used for Air Traffic Control (ATC) and extensively in airline management.

A country's airspace is divided up into zones, each of which is controlled from a centre. In a Control Centre the Controllers sit at a large panel showing maps of their area. A radar display tube shows the position of each aeroplane as a cross, alongside of which appears the aeroplane's identifying call sign.

From the flight plans filed by the pilot before take-off the ATC central computer prints a 'strip' of paper recording the main facts. These strips are placed in racks close to the controller. He can communicate with the pilot by radio and give his instructions.

Meanwhile radar stations are tracking the aeroplane and its position is then shown on the display terminal for the controller. Each alteration in course is stored in the central computer for subsequent analysis and accounting.

Airline management use computers for maintenance schedules for the aircraft; the computer keeps a diary for each plane, noting what is due for preventative maintenance and recording all spares used and defective parts replaced.

Crew rostering in large airlines can be done using the computer to ensure that crews get to required rest-stops whilst making sure that as far as possible crews end a duty-period close to their base. Seat reservations, ticketing, passenger check-in and baggage registration are functions which are almost completely undertaken by computers in most airlines.

On the aeroplane itself on-board computers are now used extensively as part of the navigation and control systems. On some aircraft the entire landing can be done without manual intervention — though most people prefer to know that the pilots are still there!

Highly computerised cockpit of the U.S. Space Shuttle.

Sea

At sea modern cargo ships may have as much computer-controlled equipment on board as an aeroplane! A cross-channel ferry includes a control room from which the engineers control the engines without needing to go into the engine-room for much of the time.

On a bigger scale the handling of a huge oil-tanker can be a tricky business. Valuable training can be given on a simulator without having to take the real ship to sea. Instructors can program the computer to produce hazardous situations for the trainee and after the session the responses can be played back and analysed. A container ship is stacked full of containers and each one is logged by a computer system noting its contents and destination. Containers can be off-loaded at the right port and (hopefully) do not get lost in transit.

Land

Busy road junctions are controlled by traffic lights. The time that the lights are changed and the duration for which they remain at red or green can be determined by the flow of traffic across the junction. Sensors by the side of the road count the traffic and the information is fed back to the computer controlling the lights. At major junctions TV cameras may be installed and human controllers can override the computers in special circumstances.

Public transport authorities — railway and bus operators, use computers for controlling their vehicles. For example, at major railway termini the final choice of platform may be computer scheduled. Sometimes computers actually control the movement of vehicles, in underground railways or in the rapid-transit systems connecting airport terminals with outlying parts of the airport.

Stay Healthy

From the day you are born until the day you die your health is recorded and monitored.

If you should have to go into hospital you should not be surprised to know that your 'stay' there is extensively recorded and tracked by computer. On your admission details about your illnesses and details such as your name, age and address are entered into the computer. While in hospital a continuous case history is built up; clinical reports, results of tests and day-to-day changes in your condition are keyed into the machine.

Hospitals also have special-purpose computers built into a host of different pieces of equipment. Modern machinery for scanning patients, such as those units which track the condition of an unborn baby, are computer-controlled.

A new approach to health care is 'AUTOMATED DIAGNOSIS'. If the patient can give enough information to a computer through a carefully devised pattern of simple questions the machine is capable of giving a diagnosis of the illness. One interesting fact that has emerged from research in this area is that patients often prefer to tell their symptoms to a machine rather than another human!

Your family doctor in his surgery is also beginning to use computers for record keeping and noting details of prescriptions given out. If a doctor notices that a particular patient is showing side-effects of a certain drug, it is possible to search the patient-records to see if other people are showing similar side-effects.

A heat thermograph reproduced on a VDU. VDU facilities aid doctors in studying the body.

The Computer goes to School

The main use of computers in education is for processing examination results!

Certificates for passing examinations are given to the successful students but behind the scenes a huge mass of facts and figures are produced to aid the education authorities.

In schools the computer can be an aid to the making of timetables — quite an exacting task which can keep a couple of teachers busy throughout the summer holidays!

Apart from timetables what are they used for? In some subjects the computers are used as calculating aids, particularly if the mathematics involved is very complex. Other subjects require databanks of information to be built up and used like a textbook. A particularly interesting area is the use of the computer as a teaching aid. Computers can be used to help people to read, for example, by flashing up a picture of an object and then its name. The pupil has to make some response and the computer can then move on to the next task or repeat the lesson. The main advantage is that the computer never gets tired or angry! The pupils learn at their own pace, but in a strict sequence.

This type of learning is called 'COMPUTER-ASSISTED INSTRUCTION' [CAI]. CAI is popular outside of school, as a way of training people in specific jobs — even in the computer industry!

Gamesters

Like the television and the video recorder before it, the home computer's main use is for entertainment. Entertainment means games!

Games have always been played, ever since the dawn of civilisation, and apart from being enjoyable they are often a means of learning something.

For example, nearly all the popular arcade games require the player to:
— think fast.
— respond quickly to movements.
— move the controls quickly and accurately.

If you don't do all these you get zapped by the aliens pretty quickly! You will find yourself becoming more accurate as you play these games; your speed of reaction will become faster and you will be able to judge the direction of an enemy missile. An important aspect of a good game, therefore, is that it can be played over and over again, giving you the chance to get better at it — if it is too easy it quickly becomes boring!

GOODIES v. BADDIES

At the moment nearly all the games available on home computers seem to be of two main sorts:

ACTION GAMES — Where you pit your wits against aliens or some other enemy and attempt to shoot them before they get you.

ADVENTURE GAMES — Where you take a particular role (such as playing the hero) and the computer takes other parts (such as monsters, ghosts, aliens etc.) and tries to stop you reaching your goal — perhaps hidden treasure or a beautiful heroine held prisoner.

The player is given a small number of 'lives' and usually the game gets harder as it progresses. It gets harder because the computer program gets faster or because additional perils are introduced. The stage at which it gets harder is often decided by the player — though he doesn't know it. As the player shoots down more flying saucers, for example, he is scoring points. When the value of points scored reaches a certain total the program introduces the things which make the game harder.

LADY LUCK

There is something else involved — chance. Luck plays an important part in the games.

How is luck programmed into a computer? A random-number generator is used. Random numbers are like raffle tickets plucked out of a hat; it is not possible to predict which number will follow which. For example, if we want to know the next number in this series: 2 4 6 8 10 ? It is fairly easy to guess that it would be 12, because the pattern of numbers is generated by adding 2 to each number in turn. But try this: 3 1 2 7 11 6 ? The next number might be anything! Suppose we want to set up a game where the computer is going to 'choose' a word that we will have to guess. All the words would need to be stored on the computer's memory

first. Let us assume that 100 words are stored. Then we would use the BASIC command: Let A = RND[x] to generate a random number for the variable 'A'. If 'A' turns out to be a number between 1 and 100 then that number can be used as the address of the memory location holding the selected word. If 'A' is outside the range 1-100 we would have to repeat the 'RND' command to get a number in the right range. The value of x is a dummy number which starts the random number generator working from a specific start point. In practice many computers generate a decimal number between 0 and 1. The programmer then has to adjust the answer from the generator if he wants to deal only in whole numbers.

Painting by Numbers

The picture is an important part of a games program.

The screen of a home computer can be thought of as made up of a number of rows [typically 20 or 24]. Each row can hold a limited number of characters [say 40].

The total number of display locations is therefore 20 × 40 which is 800. Some screens are much larger; some are smaller. You can find out the size of a home computer screen from its manual. It doesn't matter what size of TV you use with it.

The locations in the main memory, where the screen contents are stored, are collectively called the 'screen memory', and the way these are mapped out on the screen itself is very important. The memory location '1' holds the data to be displayed on the screen at line 1, character 1, i.e. the extreme top left hand corner. '800' holds the data for the bottom right hand corner.

You, the programmer, can refer to the memory positions '1' to '800' in your program and can change the contents at will. But how does the picture on the screen get there?

PAINTING BY PIXEL

Each position on the screen is called a picture element or 'PIXEL' for short. This pixel is made up of a square shape or 'matrix' of dots, each of which can be illuminated to make up the shape of the character the programmer wants on the screen.

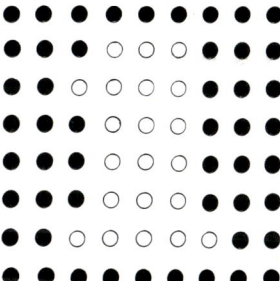

An eight by eight matrix to show '1'.

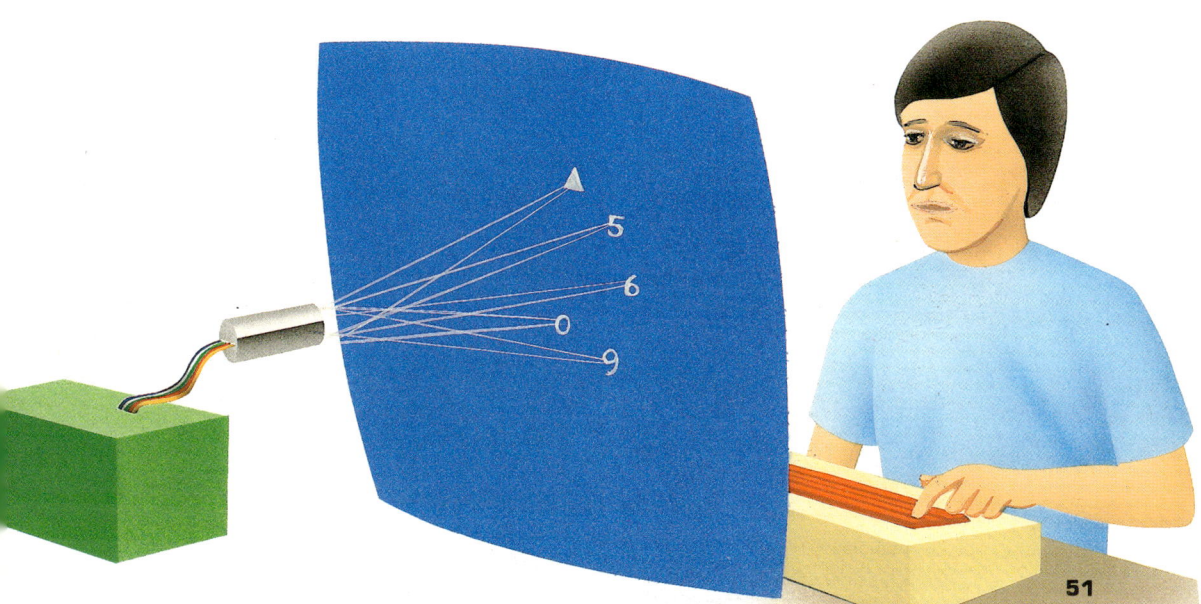

The more dots there are in the matrix the better, because it means higher picture quality or detail. We call this 'high resolution'.

The dot matrix patterns for all the characters that can be shown on the screen are stored in a separate ROM associated with the video electronics of the computer. When the programmer moves a value for, say, the character 'B' into the screen memory at, say, location '200', what is actually stored at '200' is the address in the video ROM of the location where the dot matrix pattern for 'B' can be found.

This is all right if the video ROM manufacturers have included all the characters that you might want to display! If he hasn't you are rather limited.

With 'low resolution' graphics all you are likely to get in the 'ROM' are the standard letters of the alphabet and perhaps one or two building blocks. So if you draw a picture of a person using one screen position for each graphics character and low resolution blocks you get a picture like this:

It's very simple and not very lifelike. It does have a great advantage, however, in that it requires only a small amount of storage space in the main memory.

With high resolution graphics more detailed dot matrix patterns are used and in some of the modern home computers the shapes of the characters are stored, not in the video ROM, but as bit patterns set up by the programmer in the main memory.

This has the enormous advantage that the graphics are entirely under the control of the programmer — you can design the exact shape of an alien space craft; but it uses a lot of memory space. Using a lot of main memory for graphics can mean that you have less space for the rest of the program, so computers with small memories are less useful.

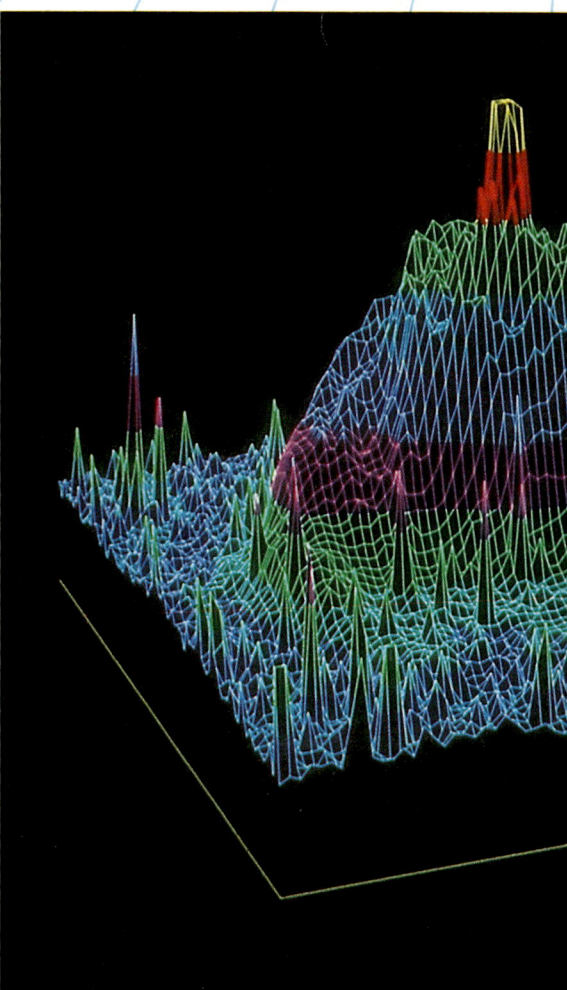

THE COMPUTER'S PAINT BOX

Colour is an important attraction for the games programmer. It is usual to provide a 'palette' of colours and to be able to mix them at will. Background and foreground colours may be decided in the program by the use of comands like PAPER and INK. These are extensions to the BASIC language and are often unique to one particular make of computer.

With the bit-mapped high resolution graphics systems the colour of a pixel is often determined by additional bit-settings in the main memory. Again this tends to increase the amount of space used by the graphics facility and thus reduces the amount of space for other things.

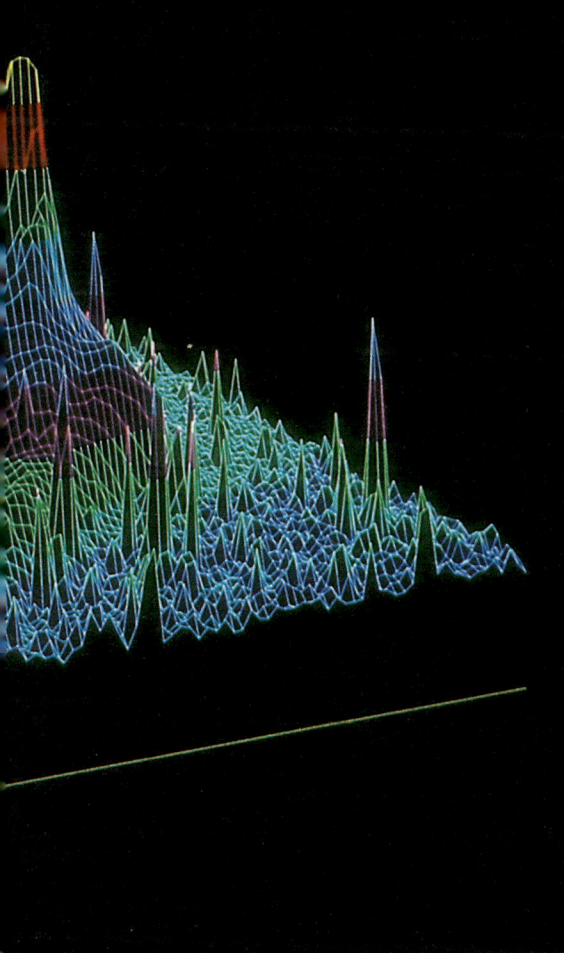

KAPOW!

What other things might you want for a realistic and exciting game? How about sound? Most shooting games use an explosion noise and other shrieks, whistles and warbles can be produced as well. A typical sound system will provide several 'tone generators' which can be sounded together to produce a chord or individually to get different notes to make computer music. A separate generator is often used to provide the 'white noise' which is the basis for game explosions.

The BBC micro has three tone generators and a separate noise channel which can produce eight specific sound effects.

The commands SOUND and ENVELOPE are used to produce different sorts of noise. The SOUND command has the format:

SOUND C, A, P, D.

C controls which channel is to be used (0, 1, 2 or 3). A is the volume and goes from 0 (silence) to −15 (loudest). P is for Pitch and goes from 0 (low) to 255 (high) and D is for duration which goes from 1 to 255 in steps of 50 milliseconds.

The ENVELOPE command is used to modify the tones produced by SOUND so that more realistic music can be produced. The really dedicated musically minded programmer will soon be using the micro as an electronic organ!

Computer graphics display of light coming from a whirlpool galaxy in space.

Tomorrow's Home

One family in twenty in the UK already has a home computer.

What would you use a home computer for? The answer at the moment, if you've just got one, is probably that you're just about to load a new games program! In other words, you are using the computer for entertainment. There is nothing wrong with that but consider for a moment all the things it might be used for in, say, ten years' time . . .

SHOPPING

It's 1995 and you need to do some shopping. You key in the code on your computer to identify the shop — perhaps a well-known supermarket. Their most recent price lists and special offers are displayed on the screen.

You have already stored in your computer the 'normal' shopping list but after browsing through the special offers you add some extra items, keying in the code if you have an old-fashioned 1980's computer. On the other hand, if you have a 1995 voice terminal, trained to recognise your voice, you merely tell the machine what the items are!

As your goods are packaged in a universal shopping basket, specially designed to fit into the delivery vehicle (no more cardboard boxes in the car boot!), the supermarket computer automatically gets in touch with your bank's computer. Your bank balance is adjusted — you've now ordered and paid for the goods and they are on their way to you, and you haven't even moved from your 1995 armchair!

Computer shopping and home-banking are already in existence in the 1980's. Using PRESTEL communications you can connect your computer via ordinary telephone lines to commercial services.

EDUCATION

You still have to do your homework but it's a mixture of re-running this morning's lesson on the video, plus a test (afraid so!) which you answer over the computer terminal. But your art homework is much more interesting because you are doing sculpture. Using the computer to help you fashion the shape, you produce a beautiful statue — you can see all round the object by moving the VDU controls. However good it looks on the screen, though, it really needs to be seen for real — or does it? You switch on the hologram projector and into the room comes a full-sized version of your sculpture.

It's science fiction, yes, but it's not that far away!

SPOT THE COMPUTER

There are probably a few computers already in your home — you might not have noticed them at all but they are there!

Do you know someone with a new sewing machine? Modern ones include a host of micro-circuitry. The internal microprocessor is programmed to create a score or more of different stitches ranging from basic straight and zig-zags to fancy decorative ones. It's the same with washing-machines and cookers.

Finally, houses themselves are becoming more automatic with control mechanisms for the heating, lighting, air conditioning and security all becoming computer-controlled. Even Grandad in the greenhouse will be using a computer to monitor the moisture content of the soil!

Tomorrow's Office

Already a larger proportion of people work in what is called the 'services sector' of our economy than in the 'manufacturing sector' where goods are actually made. More people work in offices and here the electronic revolution is well and truly under way.

Ask most people what they visualise by the word 'office' and they probably think of a room cluttered up with old desks, filing cabinets, telephones and papers.

Reality can be — but not always — very different.

It's too early to talk about the 'paper-less' office or the 'electronic' office because to most people paper is something that will always be required. However, it is possible to build an office without the need for paper — and it can be done using existing technology.

Research has shown that in a large business most of the paperwork is generated inside the business itself — perhaps in the form of memos (notes that one person sends to a colleague), company reports or in jottings of one sort or another.

But people could use a computer terminal instead of writing by hand or dictating to a secretary. The information typed into the VDU would then be sent via the computer to the person it was intended for. The computer would keep a record that the note had been sent, and when the recipient called it up on his screen to read it the computer would record that too. So he could never claim not to have received the note! This type of system is called 'ELECTRONIC MAIL'.

PROCESS IT!

One computer which is becoming increasingly important is the 'WORD PROCESSOR'. Word processing is a way of entering text information into a computer. This allows speedy correction and the printing of lots of copies. Mistakes can easily be corrected by backspacing, hitting the correct key and 'overwriting' the new character onto the screen.

Word processors do a lot more besides. Not only individual characters, but whole sentences and paragraphs can be moved about on the screen as the author decides to re-arrange the text. Unlike the traditional typewriter, which requires paper to be changed at the end of each page of text, the word processor stores all the information input as a computer 'document'. It doesn't worry about page breaks until the operator wants to print; then the word processor will chop the text up into the pages and number them as well!

An author's first draft or print-out need not be very neat but for the final version the author may choose to have the text printed with different spacing between the lines or with a different style of lettering.

With the latest word processors you can even merge separate documents by taking bits of different texts and arranging them together. Or you can add spoken comments to the text so that if you send the document by electronic mail the receiver can hear your recorded voice.

Tomorrow's World

You can't tell what the future will be, even with a computer! If you try to predict what the computer will be able to do in, say, twenty years, you could be very wrong.

Just after the Second World War a senior manager in a large corporation is said to have advised against manufacturing computers. He said the only people who could afford them would be governments and no government would want more than two or three! How wrong he was.

We can say with certainty that we are seeing the beginning of a new trend: the computer revolution. It is going to affect our lives in ways we haven't considered. Let's look at some of the changes we can expect to see.

In the future, probably within our lifetimes, we can be reasonably sure that intelligent machines will be built. If a machine can think in the way we do will it have a soul? Will it be able to feel emotions — laugh and cry? Will it write poetry and paint pictures? We know that machines can do these things already but the creative genius behind them is the programmer. When the machine doesn't need a programmer the robots of science fiction will become a reality.

Meanwhile what of mankind? What changes will we notice?

NO MONEY—SO YOU'RE RICH!

We have already seen in earlier chapters that computers are used to organise business affairs. The increasing use of cash dispensers and home computers linked to shops may lead to the 'cashless society'.

Imagine it. Only the poor would have money because they won't have access to the electronic computer systems. Robbery for money would be confined to a small section of the population but theft of information would increase. It is already estimated that COMPUTER-RELATED CRIME amounts to billions of pounds. Usually it is not real money that is stolen; it is information. If the motive of a theft is to steal money what actually happens is that the criminal tries to alter the value in his bank account by mucking about with the bank's computer!

HOMEWORK

Along with the cashless society will come the merging of the home and workplace. The office worker may be able to do most of his work from home using a terminal in the house. The worker in manufacturing industry could slowly be displaced by computer-controlled machinery.

IT'S YOUR CHOICE

In the long run any of these things may or may not happen. What we do know is that humans will decide the issue, not computers. Computers are a tool — Mankind can choose to employ them for good or ill. At the moment we are moving towards a situation where we will depend on the machines to make our society work, but we cannot say whether it will be better or worse to live in as a result.

Carry on and learn more about computers and help to shape your future!

Glossary of

A

ADA Programming language named after Ada, Countess of Lovelace.

ADDRESS Identification of a place in the computer's memory.

ALGOL Algorithmic language — commonly used scientific programming language.

ALU Arithmetic and Logic Unit — part of the CPU where data is processed.

APPLICATIONS PROGRAM Program written to do a task for a user; e.g. payroll, invoicing.

ASCII American Standard Code for Information Exchange — a method of encoding numbers, letters etc., for internal storage in the computer.

B

BACKING STORE High capacity memory; e.g. disc, magnetic tape.

BASIC Beginners Allpurpose Symbolic Instruction Code — an easy-to-learn high level language.

BINARY A number system containing only two digits, 0 and 1.

BIT A binary digit.

BYTE A group of bits (usually eight) used to represent one character in the computer. The exact pattern of bits follows a coding system (e.g. ASCII).

BUG An error in a program.

C

CAD Computer Aided Design — computer system used in engineering design.

CHIP Silicon chip — a small wafer of silicon with a metal oxide coating on which is engraved a logic circuit. Modern technology allows more and more circuits to be put on one chip.

COBOL Common Business Oriented Language — the most frequently used programming language for commercial work.

COMPILER A piece of software which converts a high level language into a machine-readable form.

CPU Central Processing Unit — the heart of the computer which controls and coordinates the other units.

D

DATA The raw material of the computer which is processed to provide information.

DATABASE Collection of useful data items used by several computer programs.

DISC A circle of plastic coated with a magnetic substance. It is used to store data or programs.

F

FLOPPY Small flexible discette often used in home computers.

FORTRAN Formula Translation — commonly used high level language.

FLOWCHART Method of showing, in the form of a diagram, one way a program will work.

G

GATE A logic gate — a switch in an electronic circuit.

GRAPHICS Name given to describe pictured information; e.g. lines, points, diagrams etc.

H

HALF ADDER Computer circuit which adds two numbers and carries the answer as output signals.

HARDWARE The parts of a computer that can be seen and touched.

HIGH LEVEL LANGUAGE A programming language which is easily written by people because it uses understandable words.

I

IMMEDIATE ACCESS STORE The computer memory; a small but very fast store attached to the CPU.

INPUT DEVICE Way of getting data into a computer.

J

JOYSTICK Input device which moves up, down and sideways. Objects on the screen can be moved around very quickly by the operator; hence the popularity of joysticks in games programs.

Computerspeak

L

LINE PRINTER Output device which prints a complete line of text in one go, rather than a character at a time.

LOGIC The reasoning behind a computer program.

LOOP Sequence of instructions in a computer program which are repeatedly followed until something occurs to make a program branch out of the loop.

LOW LEVEL LANGUAGE A programming language which is written in machine code.

M

MAGNETIC TAPE A slow-speed, high-capacity backing store for computers.

MEMORY The computer's immediate access store.

MICROPROCESSOR An entire CPU fabricated on a single chip.

MONITOR Special purpose screen that gives a clearer picture than a TV for graphics.

MOUSE Hand held input device; pushed across a flat surface the mouse's movements can be used to control a cursor on the screen.

O

OPERATING SYSTEM The basic software that provides a framework for other programs.

OUTPUT DEVICE A way of getting information out of a computer.

P

PASCAL High level general purpose programming language.

PROGRAM The set of instructions to make a computer do a useful job.

R

RAM Random Access Memory A type of immediate access store, the contents of which can be changed by new data.

ROM Read Only Memory A type of immediate access store which cannot be changed.

S

SOFTWARE General name given to all programs.

T

TRANSISTOR Successor to the valve (tube) which was the first electronic switching device. The transistor was soon miniaturised and fabricated on a chip.

TRUTH TABLE A table which describes the operation of a logic gate by listing all combinations of the input signals and giving alongside the output signal that will result for each input.

V

VDU Video display Unit.

VOLATILE MEMORY Memory (e.g. RAM) which can be changed and where the contents will be lost if the power is switched off.

W

WORD Collection of bytes — the longer the word length the more powerful is the computer.

WORD PROCESSOR Special purpose computer used for the efficient input, correction and output of text.